I SEE GOD

by
Cindy Smith

A short time ago I began using little "props" in some of my photos. Recently I used the word **hope**, at one of my sunset shoots. I had just purchased it at a store I do not get to very often. When I returned home, I noticed I did not have it. My knee jerk reaction was to look online to purchase another. When I found it, the price was three times what I had paid. I said, "Ok, God, I really like that little prop. Please let it be there when I go look tomorrow."

I looked on the beach at dawn because I thought maybe it had dropped out of my camera bag. No sign of it. I went and took photos of sunrise, then bible study, then errands. I finally made it back to the spot I'd used it late afternoon. To my delight, there it was. Exactly where I'd left it.

I wondered, "Did people see **hope**? Did they pick it up but think it was not theirs? Were they to focused on the clouds to notice it?"

I sure was glad to find **hope** right where I'd left it. On the rock, facing the sun. If you need **hope**, it's yours for the taking. Open up your heart to Jesus Christ. He is "the hope of the world." In this world we will have trouble.

John 16:33 NIV states *"I have told you these things that in me you might have peace. In this world you will have trouble. But take heart! I have overcome the world ."*

May you see that peace and hope, in the pages that follow.

I SEE GOD

by Cindy Smith

Southern Arizona Press

Southern Arizona Press
Sierra Vista, Arizona

I See God

By Cindy Smith

First Edition

Author: Cindy Smith
Editor: Paul Gilliland
Formatting: Southern Arizona Press
All Photos: Cindy Smith

Published by Southern Arizona Press
Sierra Vista, Arizona 85635
www.SouthernArizonaPress.com

ISBN: 978-1-960038-44-9

Poetry

DEDICATION

A heart of gratitude and a note of thanks to Julianne, Joan, and Miss Nora who encouraged me to keep writing.

To my Heavenly Father, who makes it happen, and to the many who have changed their address to the other side of heaven, who always believed in me.

Especially Eric.

CONTENTS

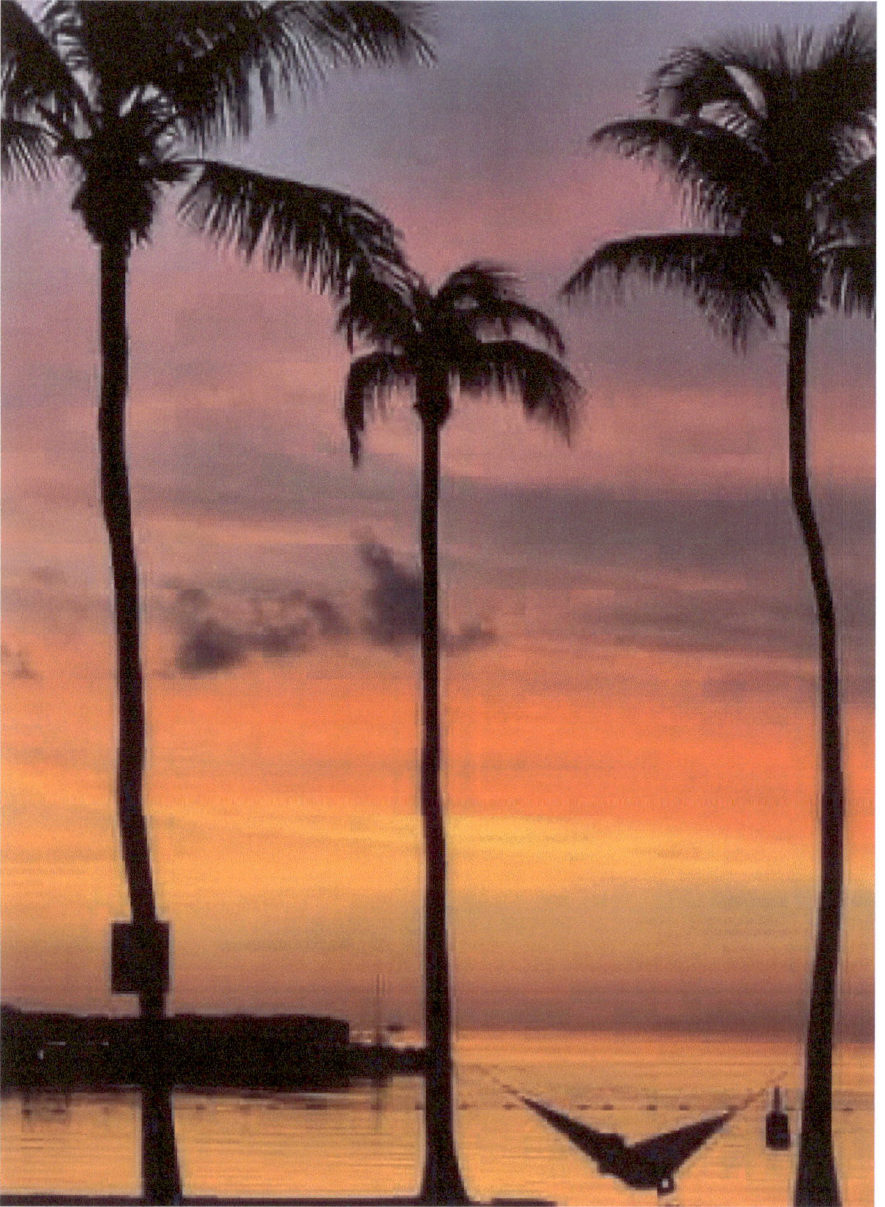

I SEE GOD

I see God in the morning
As he wakes the sun each day,
I see God as the birds fly
Their songs have much to say,
I see God in cloud shapes
Hearts and so much more,
I see God in butterflies
As they miraculously transform,
I see God in a rainstorm
In thunder and lightning too,
I see God in a rainbow
His promise to me and you,
I see God in creation
When I allow my heart
To hear his still small voice,
So, to me he can impart,
The beauty of all he has for me
The wonder of all he allows me to see.

BEAUTY FROM ASHES

There will come beauty from these ashes
Because this life is not the end,
We should be ever mindful
Of how our time we spend,
Do we love our neighbor as ourself
Or are we jealous
 of his wealth,
Do we thank the Lord every day
Whether rain or shine,
Or do we see only storms
Yet miss the rainbow behind,
His promise is never to
Leave or forsake,
His promise in the wilderness
A way he will make,
His promise is eternity
For those who trust the son,
His promise is victory
The battle is already won.

Thankful

You love me in
Unexplainable ways,
You protect me
Every one of my days,
I can find rest
Beneath your wings,
You are my strength
To do all things,
Your love never fails
Even when I do,
You give me hope
You see me through,
I can move forward
As you lead
Thankful I know
You meet every need.

HEAVEN'S GREAT GIFT

He came to bring us peace
He left his place above,
He came so we would know
Our father's immeasurable love,
The light we celebrate
That he brought here long ago,
Is a flame that burns forever
In all who truly know,
The gift that came from heaven
So, the world could see,
God's desire to love us
His heart to set us free.

ALWAYS WILL BE

As a tree standing firm
With roots planted deeply down,
Through the storm wind and rain
I am weathered but do not drown,
Part of me broken off
Many pieces gone away,
Being pruned to almost nothing
Yet planted I remain,
I ask the one who planted me
Why must I feel such pain,
Your trunk and roots will die
He says, if there is no rain,
The branches you are missing
Gave life to many things,
Shade and blossomed flowers
Perches for birds to sing,
No thing that is once loved
And part of who you are,
Ever leaves completely
It is never far,
Instead, there are reminders
Only open your eyes to see,
What was once a part of you
Still is and always will be.

LOVE LETTERS FROM HEAVEN

Love letters from heaven
Everywhere I see,
Heavenly Father
How much you care for me,
I only need to look up
Your signs are everywhere,
Every day there are cloud hearts
When I gaze up in the air,
You wrap your arms around me
To my heart you speak,
Your strength continues to lift me
Even though I feel weak,
Let me shine, let me love
Only to reflect,
Your glory and your power
That others might inspect,
You are here in the midst
Of a world that's full of grief,
You are writing to each one of us
YOU are our relief,
Thank you, heavenly Father,
For loving me so much,
Thank you, every day,
For your tender loving touch.

GREEN PASTURE DAY

I want to take
A green pasture day,
Lord please
Show me the way,
My desire
Is to follow you,
My heart yearns
To be renewed,
In the joy that I had
When I surrendered all,
In the peace that you promise
When on your name I call,
In the privilege of my father
Holding on to me,
You, are all I need
Let it be,
A green pasture day
Teach me Lord
Show me the way.

CAN'T NEVER COULD
(FOR ERIC)

When I was a young child
My momma always said,
Can't never could so often
It sure stuck in my head,
Nothing is impossible
With God and the desire,
When you put your trust in him
He will fan the flames of your fire.

Can't he never could
Even though he knew that he should,
He spent so much time doubting
That his life just passed him by,
Can't he never could
Even though he knew that he should,
Years and years of disbelief
All he could do was cry.

I knew early on that my momma
She was right,
I could do anything upon which I set my sights,
I learned to trust in the Lord
And in him to delight.

JESUS YOU'RE ALL I NEED

In these times full of uncertainty
I'm so grateful I know you're with me,
Every step I'm not alone
You are with me, while on your throne,
Holding me for comfort
Counting all my tears
Protecting me from trouble
Dismantling my fears,
Opening my eyes to seek and I have found
My savior always with me I just need to look
    around,
Leading through the valley cheering on the
    mountain top
God you are my everything and you'll never stop,
Loving caring rescuing me
When I'm lonely frightened and cannot see,
Loving caring rescuing me
Jesus you're all I need,

PERSPECTIVE

I look out as dawn begins
My emotions often spin,
Then one day to my surprise
When I opened wide my eyes,
I realized that the same event
Depending on my stance,
Looked completely different
That is not by chance,
Perspective and a different view
Will change you and reveal,
Our view and our perspective
Move us as we heal.

YOUR FRUIT IN ME

In a world that is broken filled with dismay
How can I change things show me the way,
Fleshly desires often invade
My heart that desires to persuade,
To point others to a better way
To reflect your glory every day,
May the hungry seek you may you reflect in me
The fruit of your spirit for all to see,
May I love as you love may your joy shine
    through
Spirit, give me your peace in all that I do,
May long suffering be a way to reveal
That in all things you are able to heal,
Let your kindness be evident let your goodness
    prevail
May my life reveal that your faithfulness never
    ever fails,
Let your gentleness flow through my life like a
    river
Please impart self-control let me be a giver,
Of hope that comes only from knowing you
Be reflected daily in all I say and do,
Thank you for the privilege to be
A living branch on your holy tree.

SUNSET SERENITY

Sitting here as the sun goes down
Unexpected beauty all around,
Near to me are rays of gold
Smiles appear as the light show unfolds,
How I love the peace I feel
The splendor of heaven a glimpse revealed.

HERE WITH ME

I look for you and here you are
In front of me you're never far,
Within all things your presence is
Open my eyes when I resist,
Glory surrounds me everywhere
Omnipresent you are there,
Show me things that reveal you
Show me ways to share your truth.

MORNING MEETINGS WITH GOD

The cool crisp air the beauty of the sun
Take me to a happier place my soul becomes
    undone,
Heaven is all around me I sense you oh so near
The business of life drowned out
Your voice much easier to hear,
The birds remind me gently for me you care so
    much
Keep me ever mindful do not let me lose touch,
You were you are and always will be all I'll ever
    need,
Draw me and protect me
Help me follow as you lead.

TRIUMPH OVER TRAGEDY

Triumph over tragedy grace over despair
I'm not sure where I'm going but I know that you
    are there,
Your light leads the way when I choose to
    embrace
Seeking you fully desiring your face,
You provide strength when you think I can't
    stand
You hold me close in the palm of your hand,
I thank you for loving me taking no thought
For the sins of my heart with your life they were
    bought,
Help me desire only you
Help me share all your truth,
Help me press forward let your light shine
    through,
Drawing others through my life directly to you.

MEMORY LANE

I take walks on memory lane but it's not where I
    live
These walks allow my heart to heal they have
    much to give,
Sometimes I sit and stay awhile
Often here my heart will smile,
Sometimes the walks are shorter unexpected
    things arise
Sometimes I can be frightened sometimes tears
    fill my eyes,
One thing I know for certain these walks are good
    for me
They always offer something whatever that may
    be.

About the Author

Cindy Smith resides in Islamorada, part of the Fabulous Florida Keys. She has been writing poetry since childhood. She has a published work, *Grace Through Grief , My Story His Glory*, dealing with multiple traumatic losses and how her faith continues to carry her through.

This is her first collection of poems and photos to be published in book form.

Quiet time with God in nature provides multiple canvases for photos, which in turn inspire her poetry.

Volunteering and helping the underserved both locally and globally through various organizations give her great joy.

www.ingramcontent.com/pod-product-compliance
Lightning Source LLC
Chambersburg PA
CBHW041808040426
42449CB00001B/7